D0805897

IF YOU WERE A KID ON THE
Mayflower

BY JOHN SON • ILLUSTRATED BY ROGER ZANNI

CHILDREN'S PRESS® An Imprint of Scholastic Inc.

Content Consultant
James Marten, PhD, Professor and Chair, History Department, Marquette University, Milwaukee, Wisconsin

NOTE TO THE READER, PARENT, LIBRARIAN, AND TEACHER: This book combines a historical fiction narrative with nonfiction fact boxes. While all the nonfiction fact boxes are historically accurate and true, the fiction comes solely from the imaginations of the author and illustrator.

Photos ©: 9: North Wind Picture Archives/Alamy Images; 11: National Maritime Museum, Greenwich, London; 13: Private Collection/The Stapleton Collection/Bridgeman Art Library; 15: William Attard Mccarthy/Dreamstime; 17: Chronicle/Alamy Images; 19: Stephen Barnes/Alamy Images; 21 left: Aksenova Natalya/Shutterstock; 21 center: bazilfoto/iStockphoto; 21 right: Isselee/Dreamstime; 23: SSPL/Getty Images; 25: Gregory Rec/Portland Press Herald/Getty Images; 27: State Library of Massachusetts.

Library of Congress Cataloging-in-Publication Data
Names: Son, John, author. | Zanni, Roger, illustrator.
Title: If you were a kid on the Mayflower / by John Son ; illustrated by Roger Zanni.
Description: New York, NY : Children's Press, an imprint of Scholastic Inc., 2018. |
Series: If you were a kid | Includes bibliographical references and index.
Identifiers: LCCN 2017032484 | ISBN 9780531232163 (library binding) | ISBN 9780531243145 (pbk.)
Subjects: LCSH: Mayflower (Ship)—Juvenile literature. | Pilgrims (New Plymouth Colony)—Juvenile literature. | Massachusetts—History—New Plymouth, 1620-1691—Juvenile literature. | Children—United States—History—19th century—Juvenile literature.
Classification: LCC F68 .S7688 2018 | DDC 974.4/02—dc23
LC record available at https://lccn.loc.gov/2017032484

Scholastic Inc., 557 Broadway, New York, NY 10012

1 2 3 4 5 6 7 8 9 10 R 27 26 25 24 23 22 21 20 19 18

TABLE OF CONTENTS

Searching for a New Home

England is a country that lies across the Atlantic Ocean from America. Four hundred years ago, there was one official religion there. It was called the Church of England. But some English people, called **Puritans**, wanted to worship differently. One group of Puritans called the **Separatists** left England. They spent some time in Holland. Then they decided to sail to America and build a new home. These people became the group we know today as the Pilgrims. Imagine being a kid sailing across the Atlantic Ocean. You would be on a ship called the *Mayflower*. You would share a small, crowded space with many other passengers. The voyage would be long, difficult, and dangerous.

Turn the page to board the *Mayflower* as it sails into American history. You will see that life today is a lot different than it was in the past.

Meet Hope!

Hope Smith is the middle child of a Pilgrim family heading to America. She has an independent spirit and loves to explore new places. Sometimes she gets into trouble. But mostly she makes a lot of new friends! She has been on the *Mayflower* for one week. She already knows the ship and its passengers better than the crew. Her mother is expecting a baby to be born when they arrive in America . . .

Meet Theodore!

Theodore Williams was born in Holland after his parents moved there from England. Now they are moving to America. Theodore is sad to be leaving his home in Holland. He will miss his friends. The ship that is supposed to carry Theodore's family to America is called the *Speedwell*. But the ship sprang a leak after a short time at sea. Its passengers have to squeeze onto the already crowded *Mayflower* . . .

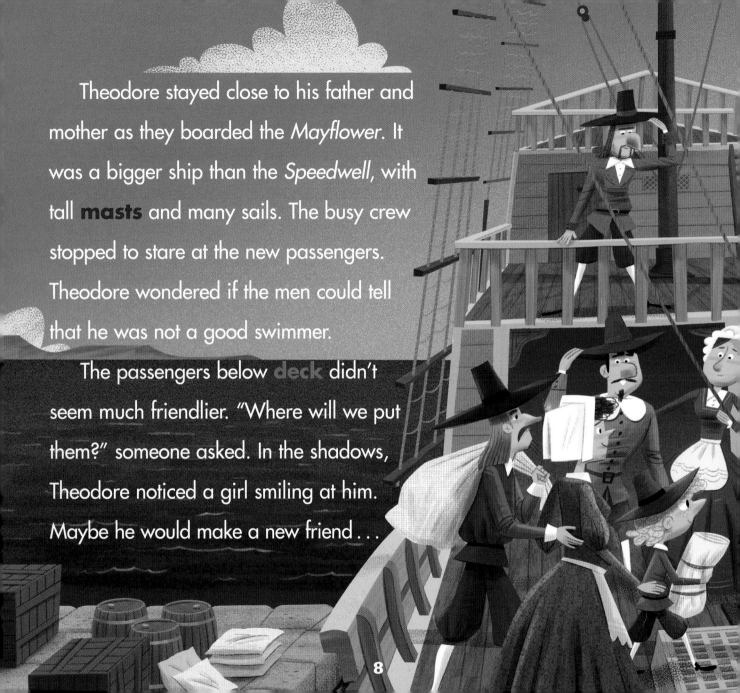

Theodore stayed close to his father and mother as they boarded the *Mayflower*. It was a bigger ship than the *Speedwell*, with tall **masts** and many sails. The busy crew stopped to stare at the new passengers. Theodore wondered if the men could tell that he was not a good swimmer.

The passengers below **deck** didn't seem much friendlier. "Where will we put them?" someone asked. In the shadows, Theodore noticed a girl smiling at him. Maybe he would make a new friend . . .

8

A RECORD OF THE JOURNEY

How do we know about the Pilgrims and their journey? A book called *Of Plymouth Plantation* tells us a lot. The book is the journal of William Bradford. Bradford was one of the Pilgrims' leaders. He writes about everything that happened at the time. The *Mayflower*'s trip across the ocean is one subject. He also writes about how the Pilgrims built a **settlement** in what is now Massachusetts.

The original of this important book is kept at the State Library of Massachusetts in Boston.

Hope saw how many new passengers were coming on board. She worried there would not be enough **provisions** for everyone. She knew what was in the ship's **hold**. She had counted all the barrels in there twice.

She saw that one of the women was pregnant like her mother. The boy standing next to her looked scared and unhappy. Hope smiled to make him feel better. She stepped forward and asked the boy what his name was.

"I'm Theodore," he said shyly.

WHAT'S FOR LUNCH?

Food choices were limited for the crew and passengers aboard the *Mayflower*. They mostly ate hardtack, a hard, dry biscuit. They also ate beef, pork, or fish. But it was heavily salted so it wouldn't spoil. The main drink was beer. This is because water stored for a long time on the ship could make people sick.

Hardtack never spoils as long as it is kept dry.

11

Hope's parents helped Theodore's family settle into the crowded space. Hope asked her new friend if he wanted to see the rest of the *Mayflower*.

"But the ship's master told us not to nose around," Theodore said.

"Don't worry," said Hope. "No one will even notice us. I know all the best hiding spots!"

NO ROOM OF YOUR OWN

The Pilgrims could not afford to travel on a passenger ship. The *Mayflower* was a small cargo ship called a carrack. It wasn't meant to carry passengers, especially for long distances. Passengers were allowed a few belongings each. There were no rooms or beds. The Pilgrims all had to share space with their neighbors.

A cutaway of a 17th-century cargo ship

Hope led Theodore through the decks of the ship. Soon, they reached the hold at the bottom. Theodore's eyes widened at the rows and rows of barrels. This was where all the food and supplies were stored. They would need these for the long voyage.

There were also all kinds of tools. Some of them were things Theodore had never seen before.

Hope noticed Theodore looking at the tools. "We will use them to build our homes in America," she said.

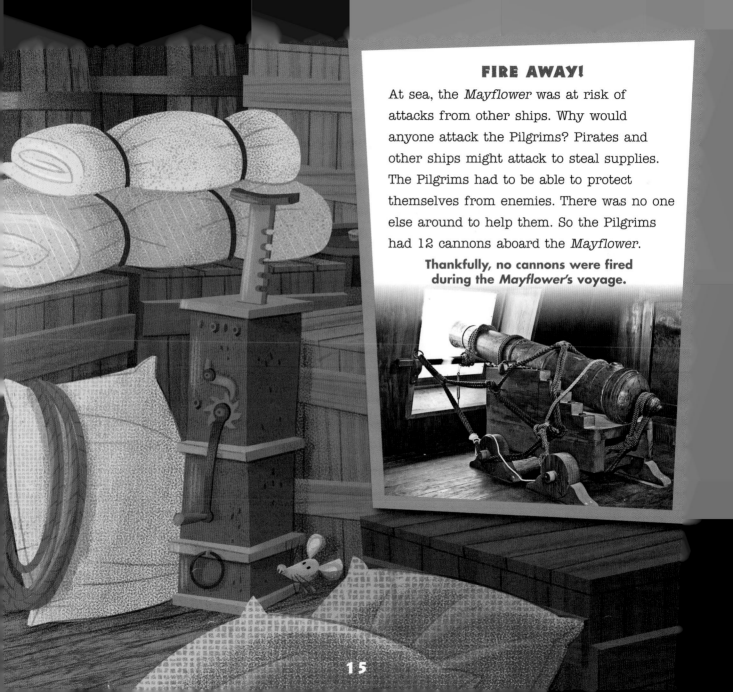

FIRE AWAY!

At sea, the *Mayflower* was at risk of attacks from other ships. Why would anyone attack the Pilgrims? Pirates and other ships might attack to steal supplies. The Pilgrims had to be able to protect themselves from enemies. There was no one else around to help them. So the Pilgrims had 12 cannons aboard the *Mayflower*.

Thankfully, no cannons were fired during the *Mayflower's* voyage.

"Let's go up on deck!" Hope said. "I want you to meet a friend."

They walked between the busy crew members on deck. Hope knocked on a wooden door. A bearded man poked his head out. "Oh, it's you," he growled. "Looking for more scraps?"

"Stubb, this is my friend Theodore," Hope said brightly.

Stubb held out his big hand. In his palm were two squares of cheese. Hope looked at Theodore. "Our moms need it," she said.

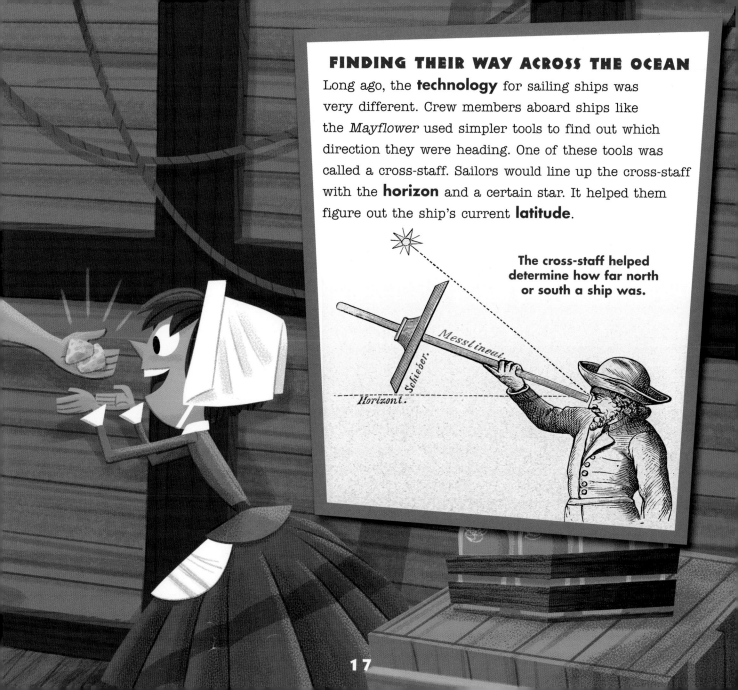

FINDING THEIR WAY ACROSS THE OCEAN

Long ago, the **technology** for sailing ships was
very different. Crew members aboard ships like
the *Mayflower* used simpler tools to find out which
direction they were heading. One of these tools was
called a cross-staff. Sailors would line up the cross-staff
with the **horizon** and a certain star. It helped them
figure out the ship's current **latitude**.

**The cross-staff helped
determine how far north
or south a ship was.**

Messlineal
Schieber.
Horizont.

A few days later, provisions were running low. Stubb continued to sneak bits of food to Hope and Theodore. They brought the food back to their mothers. The rest of the time, the two friends had little to do. They watched each other get dirtier and smellier.

One day, they were sitting in a circle of rope, counting clouds. Theodore heard the ship's master yelling. He looked out and saw the horizon growing very dark.

A crew member ran past them toward a mast.

"Get below, children!" he cried.

"It's a storm!"

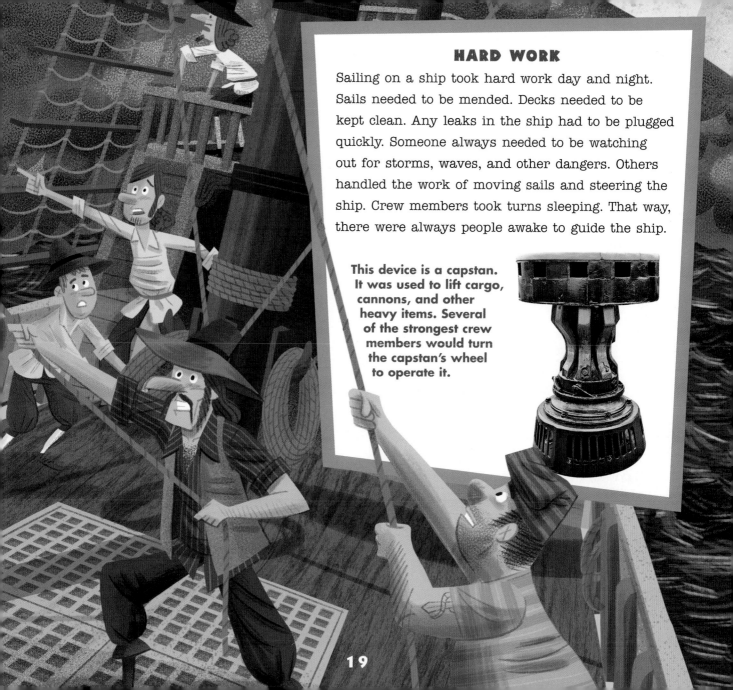

HARD WORK

Sailing on a ship took hard work day and night. Sails needed to be mended. Decks needed to be kept clean. Any leaks in the ship had to be plugged quickly. Someone always needed to be watching out for storms, waves, and other dangers. Others handled the work of moving sails and steering the ship. Crew members took turns sleeping. That way, there were always people awake to guide the ship.

This device is a capstan. It was used to lift cargo, cannons, and other heavy items. Several of the strongest crew members would turn the capstan's wheel to operate it.

The *Mayflower* sailed straight into the mighty storm. The ship was tossed about like a piece of cork. Cold ocean water poured inside. It soaked the passengers and all their belongings. Even the hold took on water. Some of the provisions were ruined.

Hope and Theodore held on to each other tightly. They felt sick, cold, and scared. Even the dogs on the ship stopped barking. The storm raged on. There was nothing for Hope and Theodore to do but wait it out. The crew worked hard to keep the ship afloat.

ANIMALS ABOARD THE SHIP

In addition to human passengers, there were also animals aboard the *Mayflower*. At least two dogs came along. One was an English mastiff, and the other an English spaniel. Pilgrim journals mention chicken broth. So historians believe chickens must have been on board, too. Some think there were also a few pigs. These would help the Pilgrims start their settlement in America.

Chickens, pigs, and dogs such as the English spaniel were important to new settlements.

Days later, the dark clouds gave way to clear, blue skies. But it was not the end. Another storm soon crashed into the *Mayflower*! Huge waves blasted the ship. The wind blew so hard that a beam snapped!

The kids joined the other passengers for an emergency meeting. They would need to repair the beam or turn back. Hope and Theodore looked at each other.

"The tools in the hold!" they both shouted.

The ship's master smiled.

"Exactly," he said.

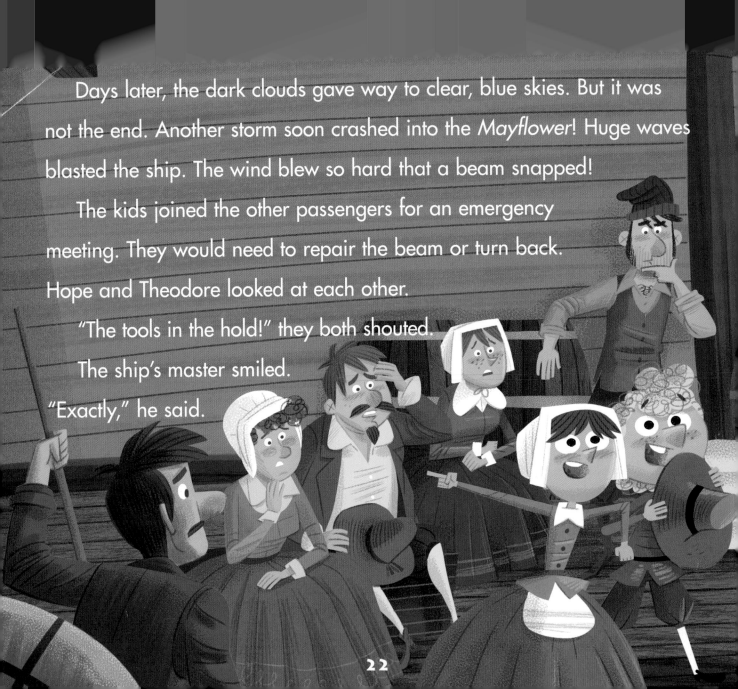

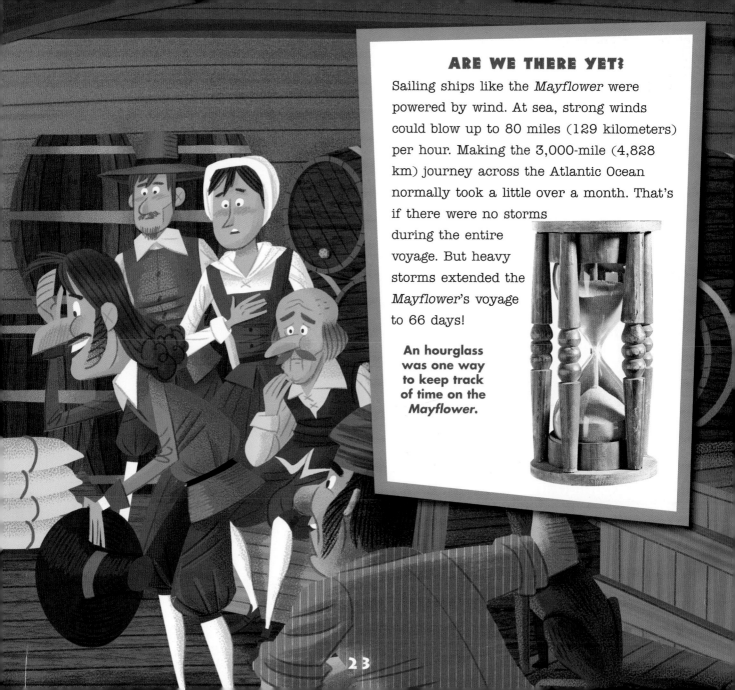

ARE WE THERE YET?

Sailing ships like the *Mayflower* were powered by wind. At sea, strong winds could blow up to 80 miles (129 kilometers) per hour. Making the 3,000-mile (4,828 km) journey across the Atlantic Ocean normally took a little over a month. That's if there were no storms during the entire voyage. But heavy storms extended the *Mayflower*'s voyage to 66 days!

An hourglass was one way to keep track of time on the *Mayflower*.

With everyone's help, the broken beam was soon repaired. The *Mayflower* was saved! "You two will make great sailors one day," the ship's master said to Theodore and Hope. He was very impressed with their quick thinking.

The ship's master told the kids they could spend the night outside on the main deck. That night, the two friends counted the stars until they fell asleep. It had been quite a day.

IN CASE OF EMERGENCY

What if the *Mayflower* had started to sink during the storm? The passengers would have had to escape using lifeboats. There was one small sailboat on the top deck called a shallop. It could carry about a dozen people. There was also a longboat that needed to be rowed by 10 to 12 men. But the two boats weren't big enough to carry all the people on board. Thankfully, the *Mayflower* never sank.

The shallop on the *Mayflower* looked like this.

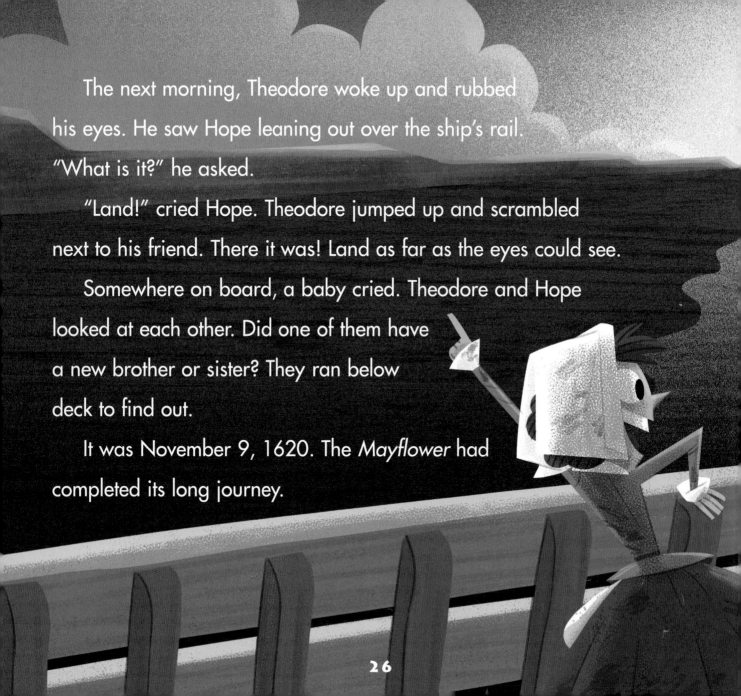

The next morning, Theodore woke up and rubbed his eyes. He saw Hope leaning out over the ship's rail. "What is it?" he asked.

"Land!" cried Hope. Theodore jumped up and scrambled next to his friend. There it was! Land as far as the eyes could see.

Somewhere on board, a baby cried. Theodore and Hope looked at each other. Did one of them have a new brother or sister? They ran below deck to find out.

It was November 9, 1620. The *Mayflower* had completed its long journey.

LIFE AND DEATH

The *Mayflower* carried 102 passengers and 30 crew members. Only one person did not make it to America. His name was William Butten. Butten was sick for most of the voyage. He died just three days before land was sighted.

One baby was born aboard the ship. He was given the named Oceanus.

William Bradford wrote a list of all the *Mayflower's* passengers.

The Route of the *Mayflower*

Plymouth,
England

Plymouth
Colony

Cape Cod

Atlantic Ocean

Timeline

1608   Separatist Puritans leave England and move to Holland.

August 5, 1620   The *Speedwell* and *Mayflower* begin the voyage across the Atlantic Ocean.

September 6, 1620   The *Speedwell* returns to port. Some of its passengers move to the *Mayflower*, and the ship leaves Plymouth, England.

November 9, 1620   The *Mayflower*'s crew spots Cape Cod just as the sun rises.

December 26, 1620   The Pilgrims finally settle in Plymouth, Massachusetts.

Words to Know

deck (DEK) the floor of a boat or ship

hold (HOHLD) the part of a ship where goods are stored

horizon (huh-RYE-zuhn) the line where the earth or ocean seems to meet the sky

latitude (LAT-i-tood) the distance north or south of the equator, measured in degrees

masts (MASTS) tall, upright poles on a boat or ship that hold up one or more sails

provisions (pruh-VIZH-uhnz) supplies of groceries or food

Puritans (PYOOR-ih-tuhnz) people in 16th- and 17th-century England who sought simple church services and a strict moral code

Separatists (SEP-uh-ruh-tists) Puritans who wanted to separate from the Church of England and worship in their own way

settlement (SET-uhl-muhnt) a small village or group of houses where people live

technology (tek-NAH-luh-jee) the use of knowledge to invent tools and devices for doing things

Index

ABOUT THE AUTHOR

John Son is the author of *Finding My Hat*, a book about his adventures growing up in Texas as a Korean American. He is also the author of *A True Book: Relaxation and Yoga*, which introduces yoga and meditation to young people. He and his family live in Brooklyn, New York, where you might run into him at a local bookstore or yoga studio.

ABOUT THE ILLUSTRATOR

Roger Zanni is a lot like Bigfoot. He is tall, hairy, friendly, and voracious. However, there are two big differences: he was raised in captivity and he loves drawing for girls and boys of all ages. He regularly creates artwork for kids' magazines, children's books, teen novels, advertisements, and anything else that might be fun and challenging from his sunny hometown of Barcelona, Spain.

Visit this Scholastic website for more information about the *Mayflower*:

www.factsfornow.scholastic.com
Enter the keyword ***Mayflower***